Poetry for Our Times

Patrick H. Williams

TEACH Services, Inc.
PUBLISHING
www.TEACHServices.com • (800) 367-1844

World rights reserved. This book or any portion thereof may not be copied or reproduced in any form or manner whatever, except as provided by law, without the written permission of the publisher, except by a reviewer who may quote brief passages in a review.

The author assumes full responsibility for the accuracy of all facts and quotations as cited in this book. The opinions expressed in this book are the author's personal views and interpretations, and do not necessarily reflect those of the publisher.

This book is provided with the understanding that the publisher is not engaged in giving spiritual, legal, medical, or other professional advice. If authoritative advice is needed, the reader should seek the counsel of a competent professional.

Copyright © 2024 Patrick H. Williams
Copyright © 2024 TEACH Services, Inc.
ISBN-13: 978-1-4796-1487-5 (Paperback)
ISBN-13: 978-1-4796-1488-2 (ePub)

Library of Congress Control Number: 2023909804

Published by

www.TEACHServices.com • (800) 367-1844

Dedication

This book of poetry is especially dedicated to my wife, Jasmine; son, Zavier; mother, Zeldina; maternal grandparents, Grace-Ann and Hezekiah; paternal grandparents Claris and Mr. Henry; and all my many family members, friends, and well-wishers.

I am eternally grateful to everyone for all the support and encouragement they have given me over the years.

With Special Thanks...

To my wife, Jasmine
For her invaluable input, steadfastness,
patience, and the many hours she spent
proofreading and
correcting the manuscript.

About the Author

Patrick H. Williams was born in St. Andrew, Jamaica, West Indies. In January of 1999 he immigrated to the United States of America. In December of 2004 he proudly became a United States citizen. He received an associate degree from Mico University, formerly Mico Teachers' College, Jamaica, in 1992. After graduating from teachers' college, he taught for two separate schools—one in the inner city and the other in rural Jamaica—for several years. He also attended Cambridge College, Boston, Massachusetts, and graduated in 2005 with a bachelor of science degree in management studies and a master of education degree with a concentration in psychological studies in June of 2022.

He has over five years banking experience with one of the top five banks in the country. He also worked for a non-profit organization in the United States of America tutoring students in the subjects of mathematics and English language arts for many years. His passion for writing began at an early age when he was in elementary school, and to date two of his poems have been published. He currently resides with his family in the state of Georgia, USA.

Introduction

P*oetry for Our Times* is a collection of original poems I have written over the years. They cover various topics, but the main theme is love, whether it is love between two human beings or two animals. At the end of each poem, I give stories of how the poems came into being and their significance to human beings. Please feel free to share with family and friends any poems that inspire you. I have been inspired by many great poems over the years which have been a tower of strength and inspiration to me at some of the most difficult times. It is my hope that some or all my poems will be an inspiration and a tower of strength to all those who read them.

Acknowledgements

To my wife, Jasmine, son, Zavier, and mother, Zeldina, who have been a tower of strength, support, and encouragement throughout this entire project, I am tremendously grateful.

To my late grandmother, Grace-Ann Messam, and grandfather, Hezekiah Messam, who instilled in me the desire to write at a young and tender age through their many stories and illustrations, I am indeed grateful.

To my late paternal grandmother, Claris Henry, and all my relatives on her side of the family, who have in one way or another influenced my life, I am eternally grateful.

To my siblings and their families, brothers Cezron, Dwight, Marvin, Lascelles, Dino, Neil, his wife, and children; and my sisters Alicia and Colleen, and their children, I am profoundly grateful.

To my mother-in-law, Ms. Hilda Bates, who brought me and my wife together.

To all those who have kept the faith with me throughout the years and impressed upon me the fact that one day I could achieve my dream of becoming a published author, I am very appreciative.

To the motivating and inspiring principal of Mico University (formerly Mico Teachers' College), the late Mr. Renford Shirley, and Professor Bill Hancock at Cambridge College, Massachusetts, who instilled in me a can-do attitude, along with my other professors, I give the utmost respect and appreciation.

To all my preschool and high school teachers including, Ms. Clark (my first infant school teacher), those at Old Providence Primary; Ms. Martin, Ms. Simpson, Mr. Owen etc. at Mona High School; I am grateful for their advice and time they spent educating me over the years.

Table of Contents

Foreword	xiii
1. Three Fingered Jack	17
2. Going for The Prize	19
3. We Love and Appreciate You	22
4. Best Thing That Ever Happened to Me	24
5. When Two People Are in Love	26
6. God's Special Gift to Me	29
7. God Bless the Day	32
8. Desire	34
9. Imagine	36
10. How Can I Ever Repay You?	38
11. I Truly Miss You	40
12. Could It Be	42
13. It's Been a While	44
14. Humble Me Lord	46
15. The Love We Have for Each Other	48
16. Thank God for Mother	50
17. Captives of Love	53
18. Life's a Jigsaw Puzzle	57
19. Who Is a True Leader	59

20. Unmasking the Real Enemy	62
21. This World Is an Unfriendly Place	65
22. Isn't It Nice to Be Nice	68
23. No Difference between Us	71
24. Let's Be Thankful for All Things	74
25. It's the Little Things That Matter	76
26. Outstanding and Upstanding Dads	79
27. The Great Reunion	87
28. Revisionist History (Standard English Version)	90
29. Revisionist History (Jamaican Creole [Patois] Version)	93
30. Sellout	97
31. Twenty-Two Years of Marriage	101
32. Don't Judge Me by My Accent	105
33. Marriage Is Not for the Faint of Heart	109
34. A True Maverick Gone, but Never Forgotten	115
35. The Quest to Be the Best	118
36. Twelve Noteworthy Original Sayings by the Author to Get You through Life	120
37. Conclusion	122

Foreword

Growing up with my grandmother, who was a Christian woman, I learned how to sing due to the fact that she was a singer and always sang. On a daily basis as a child every morning at 5:00 am, she woke me and my siblings up to have morning worship. In addition, I grew up in church and was always singing as a soloist, with my family, in choirs, in praise teams, and as a member of a group known in Jamaica as the Rainbow Singers. I remember traveling in my late teenage years with that group. We attended various churches and sang. The group was once invited to sing at a concert at a rural church. We rented a big bus and went along with our families and friends to sing at the concert. We did a sing-along as we traveled to our destination and joked around with each other. In addition, we traveled from city to city and to various rural areas, and participated in many concerts. As part of choirs and as a soloist I participated in various concerts, funerals, weddings and sang at many other special church services.

One Saturday, I was invited to sing at Patrick's church. When I arrived, he was serving as a deacon that day and stood at the front door of the church. As I walked in and said hello, he welcomed me and I found a seat and sat down waiting to sing my song. After I left his church, I never saw him again because I immigrated to the United States to be with my father.

In 1995, my wonderful grandmother, Daisy Bates, who was a devoted Christian woman and who helped to raise me, passed away. I went to Jamaica in order to attend the funeral. When my family and I arrived at the funeral,

Patrick was there to support us because he and my mom and two sisters were very good friends. After the funeral my mom introduced him to me as her church brother and a very good friend. We became reacquainted with each other. She never knew that I had met him decades ago at his church. We went our separate ways and never saw or spoke to each other until a few months later. I filed papers for my mom to come and join me in the United States. On the day she was leaving she asked Patrick to give her his phone number. He was expecting her to return to church that evening but she did not return for the evening program. Patrick, realizing that he did not see her, went to my mom's home and gave her his phone number. When my mom arrived, she told me that he was a very good Christian. She also told me he was a kind, helpful person and had a great sense of humor and was fun to be around. My two sisters spoke highly of him as their future brother-in-law. They told me that if anyone was to go to heaven, he would be going because he is a good Christian. They always tooted his horn, while all along they were setting us up and I didn't know until later.

We continued to talk casually until our conversations became more intimate and serious over time. We dated for almost two years and during those years he would write me beautiful poems of the love he had for me. On December 14, 1997 we had our destination wedding in Jamaica. He immigrated to the United States in 1999 and continued writing poems. For all these years I have been receiving poems about the love he has for me. He has also written poems on other topics including thankfulness, appreciation, joy, et cetera. We celebrated our twenty-fifth wedding anniversary on December 14, 2022. Patrick has always been a lovable, romantic man and has always enjoyed writing about the way he feels. We have weathered the storms of life together for twenty- five years and as we celebrated this milestone, our silver anniversary, we have committed our lives to each other in love forever.

Patrick is an outgoing people person and a lover of all people. He enjoys having conversations and has a great sense of humor and always makes me laugh. He's fun to be around. Whenever people are depressed, grieving, or discouraged, he cheers them up and brightens their day by making them laugh. He also writes poems to fit their occasions, whether it be a funeral, discouragement, depression, or a wedding, and gives the person the poem. He also gives family and friends hope in finding and holding onto love by telling them our story of love and sharing words of wisdom. Whenever he comes home and I have had a rough day he always does something to cheer up my spirit and tells me that he loves me with a hug and a kiss. He's a very touchy feely and sensitive man who knows what it feels like to feel people's pain when they are hurting. For twenty-five years my name has been "Honey" and he shows me that he loves me and that I am his "Honey."

Twenty-five years of marriage has taught Patrick what it means to love me and be committed to our marriage. They always say experience teaches wisdom. He has the experience to talk and write about love and also to encourage others. We have endured hardships, trials, and storms, but these experiences have taught him commitment, endurance, given him mental strength and clarity, and deepened his love for me. The storms of life over our twenty-five years of marriage have strengthened our bond, appreciation, and love for each other.

This book is encouraging, full of purpose, hope, and shows how a person can and should show love and appreciation for his or her spouse. This book is a testimony of

how my husband feels about me and he is not shy about sharing it with the world. This book means the world to me. It expresses how love can conquer and win despite pain and hardships. It shows how to appreciate, be committed, and love someone for the long term. It shows that when a man loves a woman, he can't keep his mind off her and he has to tell the whole world.
    —Jasmine Burke-Williams
    Wife of Patrick H. Williams

Three-Fingered Jack

Three-fingered Jack sat upon a rock,

Broke his back,

It was ten o'clock.

Three-fingered Jack ran down the track,

Began slipping back,

It was twelve o'clock.

Three-fingered Jack sat upon a mat,

Began sliding back,

It was two o'clock.

And if you happen to see Three-fingered Jack,

Just let him know,

Unless he stays on track,

He will most certainly fall right back into the same trap.

Reason for Writing This Poem

This is one of the first poems I have written. It began one day while I was in a creative writing class in elementary school back in rural Jamaica. The teacher told us to be creative and write something very funny. I thought for a while and then decided to put pen to paper and write the above poem entitled: "Three-Fingered Jack." My main intent was to make the poem humorous as the teacher instructed us to do.

Going for the Prize

Always be vigilant and stay focused,

Have your mind fixed on your goals,

At times it might seem unattainable,

But keep on fighting.

Support might not be forthcoming,

But it's not time to give up.

The way might appear dark, dull, and dreary,

But always look on the bright side of life.

Think positive thoughts and seek to eliminate the negatives ones.

Discouragement may come from every side,

And there are feelings,

Of making the biggest mistake of your life,

But try your best to rid yourself of these emotions.

The game might seem too competitive,

And you do not appear to stand a chance,

But this is the time to hang in there, and not throw in the towel.

Along the way there are many disappointments,

And things might not work out the way you plan,

But keep your chin up high.

Many obstacles might confront you on the road to success,

But do not allow them to impede you in your quest.

All your efforts might even seem to be in vain,

But this is not the time to quit the game.

Again, you might wonder why you chose this path,

When there are easier ways to success without the distress.

At times there might not appear to be any motivation to carry on,

But muster up all the courage you can,

With determined effort,

You will achieve your goal,

And the results will justify your steadfast determination.

Perseverance is all that matters,

Not the swiftness with which the race is run.

So be consistent.

Endure to the end.

And you certainly will win the prize.

Reason for Writing This Poem

As human beings, it is not uncommon to have setbacks, challenges, and disappointment in life. Personally, I have faced my fair share of them. I have used each of these to make me stronger, motivated, and to learn what mistakes to avoid. In fact, the words to this poem come at the end of my debut novel which is currently being edited and will soon be published. To be more precise this poem sums up some of the adversity the characters in the novel face as they go through life. The aim of this poem is to encourage all those who face obstacles in life to not give up, to keep their eyes on the goal or goals they have set for themselves, and to never stop trying.

We Love and Appreciate You

We love and appreciate you for your kindness,

We love and appreciate you for your unselfishness,

We love and appreciate you for your candidness,

We love and appreciate you for your strictness,

We love and appreciate you for your spirituality,

We love and appreciate you for your dedication,

We love and appreciate you for your faithfulness,

We love and appreciate you for your tenderness,

We love and appreciate you for your undying call to duty,

We love and appreciate you for you are truly a child of God,

We love and appreciate you for your fine and delicious cooking,

We love and appreciate you for your responsiveness,

And though these two words "love" and "appreciation" are often used but misunderstood,

We just want to say on your birthday that we love and appreciate you.

 Reason for Writing This Poem

This poem was dedicated to my wife on her forty-fifth birthday. It gives a laundry list of reasons why we love and appreciate her. It has always been a practice of mine to write poems to my wife on all occasions, but especially birthdays and anniversaries. The "we" in the poem refers to our son, Zavier, who graciously and wonderfully came into our lives in 2001. The aim of this poem was to show our love and appreciation to her for all the wonderful things she has done and continues to do for both of us throughout the years. And to be honest, she has not only done this for us, but for other family members, friends, and acquaintances.

Best Thing That Ever Happened to Me

Of all my accomplishments,

Of all my achievements,

Of all my feats,

I have been in relationships,

Some good, some not so good,

Memories I have,

Cherished and lasting memories,

The long and short of it,

You are the best thing,

That ever happened to me.

Life without you would be empty and dull,

Living without you would be meaningless,

People from time to time make wishes,

Some to live on the moon,

Others to have a dream house,

Or a luxurious car,

Perhaps great riches,

Or even long life,

But you are the best thing that ever happened to me.

And darling I want it to stay that way forever and forever.

Reason for Writing This Poem

This poem was written many years ago; it was intended to show that my wife was and still is the best thing that ever happened to me. The way we communicate with each other, put our thoughts and ideas together, and join our resources together for the betterment of ourselves, our son, families, and other people in our lives are the true sentiments I wanted to express in this poem. It is my wish that if you have carefully selected the love of your life, you can say with me, "You are indeed the best thing that ever happened to me."

When Two People Are in Love

True love is a principle,

Not just a mere feeling.

True love comes from deep within

But is often expressed outwardly.

The word love,

Occasionally misused and abused,

But when two people are in love,

There's no bound, no limit or denial.

Feelings are merged,

Impulses submerged with each other,

When two people are in love,

Though they are miles apart,

It's as if, they are right by each other's side.

Reason for Writing This Poem

Ever since the beginning of time there has been a great deal of confusion between true love and infatuation. In this poem, I wanted to differentiate between the two. True love is a principle—a principle that is wrapped up with undying love for each other and the things we love and appreciate in life and about each other. Infatuation on the other hand is based solely on feelings and emotions. While there is nothing inherently wrong with feelings and emotions since we all experience them in one way or another, the important thing to remember is that we should all be able to control them and not be so caught up in them that we are blindsided. In other words, we must not be so wrapped up in our feelings and emotions that we lose the true essence of love.

God's Special Gift to Me

You are undoubtedly,

Unmistakably,

God's special gift to me,

A masterpiece,

Directly from the hands of the Almighty.

He looks down through the annals of times,

Provided you for me, and me for you,

Then He brought you into this world,

Shaped and patterned you after His character,

And in the fullness of time,

Brought us together,

To be man and wife.

So, I cherished this day,

Every thought,

Kind deeds done,

And words spoken,

But sweetheart most of all,

It is my greatest desire,

That we will commit,

The rest of our lives together,

And ultimately inherit,

And live together in bliss,

Never to part.

Reason for Writing This Poem

As a person who was raised to be spiritually minded, I see my wife as God's special gift to me. We look forward to getting a gift or some gifts, be it on special occasions or just to have someone show appreciation to us for something we have done. We, too, may give a gift to someone for something they have done for us that we genuinely appreciate. But a gift from the Supreme is the most important gift that matters. I waited for a while to find the right person to marry. When I finally found my wife, I saw it as the best gift I have ever received. I hope you, too, someday can say that about your spouse, someone, or something special in your life.

God Bless the Day

God bless the day,

We exchange our vows,

Committing our lives,

To an endless love.

If we live,

Recognizing that with God's help,

We can accomplish what we will.

Though we know not what the future holds,

We are confident,

We can make it somehow.

So, as we begin our lives anew,

We know that many of our dreams will come through.

Let us rest our cares on God,

Who cares more than anyone else.

If we take it to Him in prayer,

We can be assured,

He will work things out.

So, put Him to the test,

And you will prove, He will always come through.

Reason for Writing This Poem

This is the type of poem that can be used in a marriage ceremony as a vow or part of a vow. It could also be part of an invitation for a wedding ceremony. It goes to the essence of what soon-to-be married couples have yearned and worked for all their lives. When I was growing up, I was often told that the things that matter to a man in life are having a career, getting married, and finding religion. I have managed to achieve these things in life and while I am not quite where I want to be, these things do bring immense joy and fulfillment to life.

 Desire

Longing,

Yearning,

Wanting desperately to be together.

Wishing,

Hoping,

Things were undeniably better.

Thinking,

Pondering,

Contemplating the future.

Controlling,

Subduing,

Restraining our seemingly unquenchable human nature.

These are some of the desires,

Two people who are in love experience,

Especially, when they are far apart from each other.

Reason for Writing This Poem

It is the human side of us to have desires. What is more important is that we must develop in ourselves the power and ability to control these desires. This poem is particularly geared toward people who are in a long-distance relationship or happen to be away from each other for an extended period. It expresses some of the emotions people go through when they are in these situations.

I, too, for a while was in a long-distance relationship. When my wife and I got married in 1997, she was living in the United States and it wasn't until 1999 when I was able to immigrate that we were truly united. I remember speaking to my wife over the phone for hours racking up hundreds of dollars in phone bills. When it finally worked out that we were together, it was the most wonderful and exhilarating thing that I have ever experienced. Then and there I could touch her and express my desire to her in a more concrete and tangible way.

Today's technology has made it possible for us to keep in close contact with our loved ones, by way of FaceTime, Skype, and other means. Even though we may not see and touch the person physically, just keeping in touch and being able to see and hear them speak goes a long way. I am especially mindful of our men and women who are in the armed services and must be away from their loved ones and families for an extended period. It is such a joy to see when these folks are reunited with their loved ones

Imagine

A gentle touch,

A passionate kiss,

The pressing together of two lips.

A warm embrace,

A penetrating smile,

Flowers,

Chocolates,

Candies and more,

Nights out,

Walks in the park,

Picnicking,

Dinner by candlelight,

And so much more,

Too many to mention,

So, stretch your imagination.

Reason for Writing This Poem

In this poem, I wanted to stretch my imagination for a while as I consider some of the ingredients that make for a worthwhile relationship and marriage. Often couples start out good in the beginning, but as the years go by and they get more familiar with each other, they stop doing the important things in life that make an enormous difference. The intent of this poem is to reignite and rekindle the sparks in the marriage relationship and to keep it going for many years to come.

How Can I Ever Repay You?

How can I ever repay you

For all the wonderful things,

You have done and said,

And continue to do?

All that I have,

Own or will ever own belong to you.

How can I repay you

For the time, effort, and energy

You have invested in this relationship,

Which has bloomed and blossomed,

In such a beautiful and enviable marriage?

While I do not seek to repay you,

With material things,

Such as silver and gold,

House, car, or land,

Or any other worldly possession,

I dedicate my love,

My loyalty,

Unwavering and undying love,

But most of all my fidelity.

Reason for Writing This Poem

This poem is based on the love and appreciation I have for my wife for all the things she has done for the almost twenty years we have been married. If you are truly honest with yourself, you will agree with me that there are many people who have impacted your life directly or indirectly over the years who you can never repay. In fact, many of the people who have impacted our lives we could never repay in dollars and cents. I have found that just simply and genuinely expressing a wholehearted "thank you" will often suffice. If that is all you can say, then say it. The bottom line is that it must always come from the heart. My wife and I have used this in our marriage over the years and it has worked wonders in our relationship. Additionally, we have learned to love and appreciate each other more and more.

I Truly Miss You

There is no doubt,

That I deeply miss you.

In fact, I cannot do without you.

You give me purpose and meaning for living,

And that is why, I am happy

You are my wife.

Every moment we spend together,

Every moment we share with each other,

Gives new meaning,

And there is absolutely no one who can pull us apart,

Not now or ever.

Reason for Writing This Poem

All of us, at some point in our lives, go through that experience when we deeply miss someone. This poem seeks to express some of the emotions people go through when they miss a loved one. While the poem, in and of itself, might not cover all the emotions that a person goes through, it touches on some that are common to all people. The point of being away from each other, especially when two people are truly in love, will cause them to feel that separation from each other. I seek to capture some of those feelings in these words.

Could It Be?

Could it be

We're a match made in heaven,

Or just two fools,

Who happened to fall in love?

Some people say,

If you fall in love,

You are most likely,

To fall out of love.

But we are in love,

And there is no second guessing about it.

Was it love at first sight

Or a union that was destined to succeed?

But once the Almighty is all part and parcel of it,

Then there is no guessing,

It will stand the test of time.

Do we have a mutual understanding between us

Or are we living in a fool's paradise?

But we complement each other so much,

Think alike in so many ways,

In so many instances and on so many issues.

Could It Be?

Was it providence that brought us together

Or was it a mere coincidence?

Ever since we met each other,

We have ample evidence

God ordained this union,

For His honor and glory.

So, let us continue to work together,

As husband and wife should do,

Knowing this for sure,

Despite all our questions and concerns,

God Almighty,

Will certainly see us through.

Reason for Writing This Poem

This is a poem in which I seek to ask a question and then answer it right afterward. On one hand, it asks the question, *could it be?* It points out some of the misconception about love out there and then presents an argument to refute them. It concludes by saying one of the true tests of love is for married couples to work together and genuinely love and appreciate each other.

It's Been a While

It's been a while since I last wrote you a love poem.

It's been a while since I bring you flowers.

It's been a while since I truly tell you how much I love you.

It's been a while since I show my appreciation,

For all the wonderful things, you have done.

It's been a while since I sincerely thank you,

For bringing our child into this world,

It's been a while since I truly show my gratitude to you,

For helping me to achieve my goals and aspirations.

God knows it's been a while.

Just simply wanting to say,

I'm proud of the day you came into my life,

And we are assured,

Prospects for the future looks brighter and better.

Than they have ever been before,

And the future looks great on every hand.

Reason for Writing This Poem

This poem has me coming full circle. I wrote it for my wife during our thirteenth-wedding anniversary. Like all couples, I get caught up in the business of life and slip up and forget to do the things I promised that I would do. So, I decided to write her a poem expressing the way I feel and apologize for not living up to the things I promise. You too might want to do a little re-evaluation and endeavor to rekindle the fire in your marriage.

Humble Me Lord

Humble me,
Humble me,
Humble me Lord,
When I get cocky,
And seem to get ahead of myself,
Humble me Lord.

Humble me,
Humble me,
Humble me Lord,
When I think too highly of myself,
Forgetting about Who it is,
That got me to where I am today,
Humble me Lord.

Humble me,
Humble me,
Humble me Lord,
When I get impatient,
And am unwilling to wait for God,
To carry out His will in my life,
Humble me Lord.

Humble me,

Humble me,

Humble me Lord,

When I get the false impression,

That everything in this world,

Revolves around me,

Humble me Lord.

When I seem not to care about anything else or anyone else,
    but myself,

All I ask,

Is that You please humble me Lord.

 **Reason for Writing This Poem**

This poem in the true sense of the word is a prayer, but it could also be used as a song. It came about one day when I was reflecting on my life, and I saw the need to get back to basics and be humble. The world today needs more people who are humble—people who will take the high road rather than flying off the handle and getting themselves in terrible and regrettable situations.

The Love We Have for Each Other

Words cannot adequately express the love we have for each other.

All the great love songs put together cannot sufficiently explain the love we plan to share with each other.

Numerous books, movies, plays, and songs have been written about love,

But none can sufficiently sum up the love we have for each other.

Philosophers throughout all ages and walks of life have come together to decipher the love we have for each other.

But none could come up with a proper explanation of the love we have for each other.

The love we have for each other is no ordinary love.

It's an extraordinary love!

And this one thing I know for sure,

The love we have for each other,

Will certainly last forever.

Reason for Writing This Poem

This poem was written for my wedding day in 1997. I put the finishing touch on it on my way to the ceremony. It was given as part of my speech to my wife. I must admit that when I wrote the words to this poem, I did not fully comprehend what I was writing about at the time. It has proven to be that every word and line in this poem is exactly true about our relationship and what we intended it to be in the future.

Thank God for My Mother

For my mother who gave birth to me,

I give God thanks.

For my mother who nurtured me,

I give God thanks.

For my mother who cared for me,

I give God thanks.

For my mother who listened to me during the most difficult and perplexing times of my life,

I give God thanks.

For my mother who nursed me and brought me back to full health when I was sick,

I give God thanks.

For my mother who has been there for me when the goings got tough,

I give God thanks.

For my mother who consoled and comforted me during the most difficult times of my life

I give God thanks.

For my mother who continues to pray, never gives up on me, and always assures me,

"Son, you can do it and make it."

I most certainly give God thanks for my mother.

Reason for Writing This Poem

It would be remiss of me to write a book of poems and not give tribute to my mother, the other woman in my life. I wrote this poem especially for her a few years ago, on Mother's Day. You should have seen the glee on her face when I framed it and finally handed it to her along with some other gifts from my wife, son, and I that we prepared for her. It serves to thank her for all the wonderful things she has done and continues to do for me. Whenever I visit with her, I see the framed poem proudly hanging up in her room. Every time I talk to her, she makes me laugh. In fact, over the years, no matter what is happening with her or going on in her life, I have found her to be a jovial person. The poem also serves to thank her for giving me confidence and a can-do spirit. All that I am and ever will be, I attribute it to my mother. Finally, this poem is a tribute to all the great mothers in the United States and throughout the world who have been a splendid example to their children and have stuck with them through thick and thin.

Captives of Love

Strolling through the thick woods,

Scampering over jagged rocks,

Navigating dense shrubs and bushes,

Suddenly he comes upon something,

That immediately captures his attention.

Drawn to each other like pieces of magnets,

Unaware they are the targets of a dragnet.

There dangles before their eyes,

Something, that is full of surprise.

But more important to him is his mate,

Who beckons him to play and partake.

And as he pauses a while to reflect,

On all the things, he has not accomplished yet,

Of many trophies he has gathered in his time,

But none compares to the one he is looking at, all so fine.

Sniffling, snuffling, and snorting,

He surveys the landscape around him.

Meantime hunters wait in eager anticipation,

Anxious to carry out their master invention.

And they make bets amongst themselves,

Two for the price of one or something else.

Yet unaware of the danger that lurks ahead,

The poor warriors go in search of their bread,

Darting forward to claim their prize,

Not realizing it would cause their demise.

A swift pulling of the ropes,

The net falls over,

At that moment, their hopes appear to go up in smoke.

And while their captors jeer and laugh and chatter,

These two cheetahs' hopes seem shattered.

Now as they journey in a cage towards the illustrious city,

Destined to spend their lives in captivity,

A showpiece for all to see in their new home,

Never to part.

Reason for Writing This Poem

As a young child, I grew up among animals while living with my grandparents in rural Jamaica. One thing that has been abundantly clear to me observing the animals is that they pretty much care for their loved ones even as humans do, and in some cases, even more. I have witnessed goats become overly concerned for their offspring when they go missing or become ill. I witnessed hens go into panic mode when predator bird swooped down and captured one of their newly hatched chicks. "Captives of Love" is another poem along the theme of love, but this time as it relates to the animal kingdom. The two cheetahs in this poem found themselves captured and in captivity, but would spend the rest of their lives together. I hope you will enjoy it and will capture something from it that will be a lasting lesson in life.

Life's a Jigsaw Puzzle

Life's a jigsaw puzzle,
   Put the pieces together,
      If you can,
         And it will finally make sense.
Life's a jigsaw puzzle,
   If one piece goes missing,
      It throws the entire thing out of balance.
Life's a jigsaw puzzle,
   If you start out down the wrong path,
      Chances are, you will never get a second chance to start over again.
Life's a jigsaw puzzle,
   If you do not have a clue as to what you are doing,
      Chances are you will never finish,
         Become frustrated,
            And finally give up.
Life's a jigsaw puzzle,
   If the pieces are lined up right,
      Your final product will be out of sight.
Life's a jigsaw puzzle,
   If you have a great deal of help and support,
      You are likely to finish fast and breathe a sigh of relief.

So, life's a jigsaw puzzle,
   Even though time consuming to perform
      In the end,
         It will be worth it all.

Reason for Writing This Poem

In this poem, I endeavor to compare life with a jigsaw puzzle. I have noticed people put together a jigsaw puzzle over time, sometimes even over years. It is a painstaking and time-consuming process. At first, when you look at the various scattered pieces all bundled together you wonder if the person will ever be able to put them in order to make sense. They put one piece in and decide this does not fit. Then they put another until they have the right one. If they know what they are doing and follow the rules of the jigsaw puzzle, then they are likely to finish in a reasonable time. If they get help, depending on whether the other person or persons know what they are doing, it could work to their advantage or help to speed up the task. Some people prefer to work alone when they are doing the jigsaw puzzle because it lessens the confusion. The goal of the puzzle is to have one final product that looks beautiful to the eyes. Life in more ways than one can be compared to a jigsaw puzzle. The major difference between the two is that in life all the pieces are not given to you at the outset but may come along as time goes by. Sometimes they fall in place perfectly and at other times they do not. But as one perseveres and endures, they will find that in the end, the pieces fall in place exactly as they should.

Who Is a True Leader?

Often, I ask myself the all-important question,

"Who is a true leader?"

A true leader is someone,

Who does not listen to gossip and rumors,

But weighs the facts for themselves.

A true leader is one apt to listen and learn,

But not quick to condemn and broadcast what is not so.

A true leader leads by example,

And does not subscribe to the notion,

"Do what I say, but not as I do."

A true leader respects everyone's opinion and point of view,

And never seeks to put anyone down.

A true leader rightly divides the word of truth,

And is not subjected to every whim and fancy.

A true leader does not seek to satisfy the majority if they are going down the wrong path,

But will stand his or her ground though it makes him unpopular and fall out of favor with some people.

A true leader has backbone and is ready to stand his ground when it comes to principle.

A true leader is a good listener and communicator,

And does not take anyone or anything for granted.

A true leader is impartial and shows no favoritism towards anyone.

A true leader stands up for what he believes and is not afraid to make it known.

A true leader will stand the true test of time,

When everything else fades away.

A true leader must be humble,

Willing to apologize whenever and wherever necessary and admit they are wrong when it is discovered to be the case.

A true leader must reveal the truth and not try to conceal the facts.

A true leader must most certainly exert a lot of influence, but rather than glorifying him or herself, will use it for the betterment and to uplift mankind.

Reason for Writing This Poem

As a management student, I have read, researched, and discussed on numerous occasions the question of who a true leader is. In fact, my thesis in college was what goes into making a great leader. One day the thought occurred to me, *Why not write a poem on who is a true leader from people I have observed and interacted with in all spheres of life.* These people seem to have the qualities of a true leader. One of the great leaders of our time is Warren Edward Buffett from Berkshire Hathaway. He is highly regarded as an American business magnate, investor, and philanthropist. Born August 30, 1930, he is currently the Chief Executive Officer of the Berkshire Hathaway Group of companies. He has been married to his wife, Astrid Menks, since 2006. He is the father of three children, two boys and one girl. He is one of the most successful and highly regarded businessmen in the United States and throughout the world.

If you are in a leadership position, I hope you will take something from this poem that will help you not only to be a successful leader, but a true leader as well.

Unmasking the Real Enemy

Oftentimes, the real enemy is lurking in your path,

But you are unable to recognize his presence.

Oftentimes the real enemy,

Pretends to have some good intentions,

But you are unable to put your hands on his true motives.

Oftentimes, the real enemy,

Conjures up all sorts of schemes,

But you cannot tell exactly what he is up to in his plans.

Oftentimes the real enemy enrobes himself,

As someone with good intentions and motives,

That you can hardly tell the difference.

Oftentimes the real enemy comes in human form,

But you cannot really tell that he is in the deception business.

Appearance you see can be deceiving.

Oftentimes the real enemy appears as an angel of light,

And you get fooled by what he does or says.

Oftentimes the real enemy antagonizes and terrorizes those who are good,

But you really cannot tell he is behind the affliction and persecution.

Since his goal is to appear to work on human behalf and in their interest,

Oftentimes the real enemy camouflages himself,

So, that he takes on the appearance of his environment,

And you cannot see him, for who he really is supposed to be.

And while the real enemy is oftentimes difficult to figure out,

It's his antics that usually give him away in the end.

Reason for Writing This Poem

Try as we may, none of us knows who the real enemy is. Some even go as far as to say the real enemy lies in all of us and not outside of us. While this is true to some extent, I have come to realize that the real enemy is an outside force that we often invite in or allow to take possession of us by way of our own decisions and outlook in life. This poem endeavors to unmask the true enemy and how he seeks to impact our lives, if we allow him to do so. Notice how he comes in disguise and seeks to impose his will on us.

This World Is an Unfriendly Place

For those of us who stand on the side of principle,

This world is an unfriendly place.

For those of us who stand on the side of justice,

This world is an unfriendly place.

For those of us who stand on the side of righteousness,

This world is an unfriendly place.

For those of us who stand on the side of integrity,

This world is an unfriendly place.

For those of us who stand on the side of freedom,

This world is an unfriendly place.

For those of us who stand on the side of fairness,

This world is an unfriendly place.

For those of us who stand on the side of truth,

This world is an unfriendly place.

For those of us who stand on the side of honesty,

This world is an unfriendly place.

For those of us who stand on the side of peace,

This world is an unfriendly place.

For those of us who stand on the side of good will to all men,

This world is an unfriendly place.

For those of us who stand on the side of morality,

This world is an unfriendly place.

For those of us who stand on the side of equality towards all human beings,

This world is an unfriendly place.

And even though doing the right thing,

May make you seem weird and lonesome in this world,

You should stand up and be counted among those that have made a lasting and impactful difference,

And just maybe, just maybe, someday, this world will become a friendly place.

Reason for Writing This Poem

There is no doubt that there are a lot of good people and good things that are being done in this world. But on the other hand, if you stand up for what is right and fair for all mankind, this world can indeed be an unfriendly place. In this poem, I try to point out how if someone stands up for what is right and just for all mankind, this world can become an unfriendly and lonesome place. Some of the most impactful people throughout life, who have stood for principle and fairness, have found this place to be an unfriendly and lonesome place. Chief among them are Mahatma Gandhi, Nelson Mandela, and Rosa Parks, to name a few. For some of them, it cost them their lives. However, the impact and legacy they have left behind will be with us for many years to come.

Isn't It Nice to Be Nice?

In a world where people have often set aside the common niceties of life,

Isn't it nice to be nice?

In a world where people often and deliberately forget to express gratitude,

Isn't it nice to be nice?

In a world where there is seldom any regard for human life,

Isn't it nice to be nice?

In a world where people are often self-centered,

Isn't it nice to be nice?

In a world where doing good is often seldom regarded,

Isn't it nice to be nice?

In a world where each is for his own and anything goes,

Isn't it nice to be nice?

And even though being nice is often frowned upon and derided,

For the world to be a better place,

It's still indeed nice to be nice.

Reason for Writing This Poem

In my earlier years, I spent time in rural Jamaica. One of the first things that I'm reminded of was how people knew, greeted, and looked out for each other. My now deceased grandparents saw to it that I assisted the senior citizens in the community and sought to help those who were less fortunate in life. I remember my grandmother instructed me to stop by an older gentleman's home in our community to check on him and help him when he needed it. She also instructed me to bring eggs from her hens for him. I was also given the task of checking on another older lady and told to assist her if she needed anything from the grocery store. I remember how appreciative she was when she gave me the money and asked me to purchase her favorite biscuits or some other items that she so desperately needed. That remains with me even to this day, and I cannot help greeting people when I see them or offering to help them in one way or the other. Also, because of that it has instilled in me a special caring and love for those who are elderly, young, and less fortunate in society up to this day. What disappoints me most of all are those people who act rudely or abruptly, and even outright refuse to show kindness when you act nice to them. It was out of this observation that I penned this poem. I hope it will influence all people to act kind towards their fellowman.

No Difference between Us

We all come from the same common ancestry,

We all have the same blood running through our veins,

So, there is no difference between us.

We all go through various hardships and challenges,

We all go through the same pain,

So, there is no difference between us.

We all have our ups,

We all have our downs,

So, there is no difference between us.

We all have our disappointments,

We all have heartaches and headaches,

So, there is no difference between us.

We all have our good times,

We all have our bad times,

So, there is no difference between us.

We all have our days of triumph,

We all have our days of rejection and disappointment,

So, there is no difference between us.

We all make good decisions,

We all make bad decisions,

So, there is no difference between us.

We all have our days of rejoicing,

We all have our days of sorrow,

So, there is no difference between us.

We were all born as babies,

We all grow old and die one day,

So, there is no difference between us.

We all suffer illness and diseases,

We either recover or die,

So, there is no difference between us.

And anyone who wants to argue,

That there is a difference between us,

Tell them this, when we die, we all go back to the earth from whence we came,

And there is absolutely no difference between us.

Reason for Writing This Poem

This poem seeks to emphasize that as human beings there are absolutely no differences between anyone of us. We experience the same things. We go through the same disappointments and heartaches. We make good or bad decisions, right or wrong choices, and we either learn from them or suffer the consequences. We get sick. We go to the doctors. They try to help us through the procedures they perform or the medicines they prescribe. Chances are we recover, but we may ultimately get sick and die. We were all born as babies from our mother's womb. We may achieve great wealth or fame or be subjected to a life of poverty. We may even dedicate our lives to helping humanity. But ultimately one day we will die. We will go back to the earth. In conclusion, there should be no distinction between any of us. We should all live in peace and harmony and learn to love one another because in the true sense of the word there is absolutely no difference between any of us.

Let's Be Thankful for All Things

For the food we eat,
For the clothes we wear,
For the roof over our heads,
For the money in our bank accounts,
For the car we drive,
For a warm place to sleep,
Let's be thankful for all things.

For the friendships, we have made through the years,
For the good influences, we have passed on to others,
For the good times, we have shared with them,
For the love, we have passed on to those we meet,
For the good days and the bad ones,
For the happy times and sad ones,
Let's be thankful for all things.

For the good people who have come into our lives,
For those who have impacted us for good,
For the beauty of the earth,
For the graciousness of nature,
For the beautiful flowers and the bountiful trees,
For the great expanse of rivers, seas and oceans,
Let's be thankful and learn to appreciate all things.

# Reason for Writing This Poem

As human beings, there are so many things which we take for granted daily. The sole purpose of this poem is for us as human beings to start showing appreciation for the things we have in life. We should realize that many people in this world are not fortunate to have some of the things we have and share. This leads me to another point: every opportunity we have, we must share with others who are less fortunate in society. For emphasis, we need to be grateful for the things of nature and learn to appreciate the things that are necessary for the preservation of life.

It's the Little Things That Matter

It is time for us to show regard for the little things in life.

Because it's the little things that matter,

Because it's the little things that count,

Because it's the little things that are impactful,

In fact, it's the little things that people talk about.

It's the little things that bear significance,

It's the little things that make life easier.

What if we fail to value the little things in life?

The little things won't matter,

The little things won't count,

The little things won't be impactful,

They won't be things that people talk about.

In fact, they won't bear any significance,

And they won't make life any easier.

Reason for Writing This Poem

Throughout life, I have found that there are things we consider unimportant but that make life easier and more bearable. Saying *thank you*, or *good morning*, or just acknowledging someone who speaks to you makes a big difference. A little laughter will brighten up your day and relieve stress. Admiring the things of nature and learning to appreciate and value them will go a long way in enhancing your mind. You may be having a bad day, but that does not prevent you from acknowledging your fellowmen. I understand we all need some alone time, but I have learned in life that the simplest of things in life can bring joy. The purpose of this poem is to help everyone to acknowledge the simple things in life which we often take for granted. These are the things that will make a big difference in the long run. So, let us learn to value the unimportant things in life and when we learn to do so we will appreciate life for what it is worth.

Outstanding and Upstanding Dads

From the beginning of time, throughout history and all over the globe, there have always been outstanding and upstanding dads.

Dads who are providers, protectors, and a powerhouse to their families, community, society, and country.

Dads who never reneged on their promises; however, they are forthright and determine that all things go well and smoothly.

Dads who are faithful, honest, trustworthy, and put family first above everything else.

Dads who love their children and endeavor to see them become successful human beings, contributing to the growth and development of themselves, others around them, and the society at large.

Dads who work extremely hard alongside their spouse for the betterment of their immediate and extended family.

Dads who are selfless and put family interest above everything else.

Dads who are not just mere sperm donors but are actively involved in their children lives.

Dads who make time, so that their wives and children can have fun, enhancing and prolonging the family's health, well-being, and longevity.

Dads who are analytical, forward thinking, and put in place plans and measures so that the well-being of the family are taken care of immediately and for many generations to come.

Dads who are eternal optimists, have a never-say-never attitude even through challenges, obstacles, discouragement, and disappointment which are likely to occur from time to time.

Dads who endeavor at all costs to raise their children in the right and proper way thereby enabling them to become useful members of their home, community, society.

Dads who contribute to the advancement of society in a positive way.

So, on this Fathers' Day and going forward, let's give special tribute, express acknowledgment, appreciation, and a big thank you to all the outstanding and upstanding dads within the borders of our country and throughout the entire globe.

Reason for Writing This Poem

I was moved to write this poem due to the fact that even though my dad was a great provider and protector of his family, I looked to other persons in my life such as my maternal grandfather, affectionately called "Hezzy" (now deceased), and the husband of a cousin of mine affectionately called "Reds" as role models. Early in life when my family had to split up due to the separation of my mother and father, my two siblings and I went to live with our grandparents in rural Jamaica. I was so excited to meet them. I remember my grandmother saying this to me: "When it comes to discipline, especially when children fall out of line and everything fails, Grandpa's hand goes up light and comes down heavy." As a child, I did not fully comprehend what she was saying but later it became clear to me. I later found him to be one of the most kindhearted, loving people one could ever find. Many times when grandfather took us to the market on Fridays, he stopped at his favorite restaurant and bought all of us our favorite breakfast. He encouraged us to work hard in school because he did not have the opportunity to attend school and neither could read or write. He encouraged us to come out to something positive in life.

He loved his younger brother. This brother, at a young age, travelled to England to participate in a war that involved Britain and other countries. As soon as there was a job opening in the Forest Department, my grandpa—who was a go-to guy in his community and known to many politicians and dignitaries— was offered a job as a forest manager. Rather than taking the job for himself, he recommended that his younger brother get the job. His reasoning was that he had finished growing his children and his younger brother was just raising his, therefore he needed the money more than he himself did. I remember year after year grandpa cleared land next to his farm, tilled the soil and planted crops on it. He would often tell us that a portion of the farm was for his service member brother and no one should touch it. When it was time to reap the crops, he placed it in bags and either took it to his younger brother's house or had me take it over to him. When his baby brother died, with whom he shared an undeniable bond, he was very heartbroken. He did his part to ensure he had a proper funeral. He was there for the family throughout and never left their side.

My mom shares with me that her father lost his mom, with whom he was remarkably close, incredibly early in life. This impacted him for the rest of his life, and he took a vow to care for his dad and siblings. There were four boys and one girl. They only could afford to have one pair of shoes. Their shoe size was around the same size so whenever any one of them had to go to an event that person took the pair of shoes. I remember granddad sending me to visit each and everyone one of his siblings during the time I lived with him. They lived a great distance from each other but from time to time, I either had to go drop something off, checking in on them and their family, or pick up something from them. Finally, he was a great provider not only for his children, but other adoptive children he and his wife raised, and also to us, his grandchildren. It was he who taught me to make cornmeal porridge without having lumps inside it. I remember when I attended Mico University (formerly Mico Teachers' College) everyone wanted me to make porridge for them since I was the only guy who could make the porridge without any lumps in it. I would often attribute it to the fact that it was my grandfather who taught me to make porridge. Everybody loved him in the community and often he would volunteer to do something for them without even charging them. Indeed, my grandfather was an outstanding and upstanding man and later when I became a father, I sought to emulate him.

Another person who I witnessed the true sense of fatherhood in was my cousin Maisy's (now deceased) husband, Reds. His parents were of German descent. The first time I met him was when my cousin was pregnant with twins. She came to live with us for a while to ensure that she had a smooth delivery. I remember him visiting her. He kissed her and kissed her belly in appreciation of the twins she was carrying for him, a daughter and a son. As a boy, I observed this with glee and wondered when my day will come when I would grow up, get married, and do the same. He also brought us delicious food from his farm such as escallions, carrots, melons, etc. I also got a chance to meet my cousins for the first time, whom I was delighted to see. Unfortunately, my cousin lost her daughter when she gave birth, but her son survived. The impact her husband left on me has lasted for the rest of my life. When I got married, I sought to emulate him to be the best dad I could be. I remember taking our son off my wife's hands so she could get some rest. I changed him, fed him, burped him, and put him on my stomach. I felt his little heart palpitating and fell asleep with him lying on my stomach on numerous occasions.

Throughout my entire life I have tried to be the best dad I can be. I taught him to be responsible, independent, and a go-getter and my wife and I took him out to many places on numerous occasions. My goal was to train him to be the best young man that he could be and when he grows up to be a husband to be the best one he could be. Indeed, there are numerous outstanding and upstanding fathers across the globe and this poem seeks to acknowledge them and to entreat them to continue to do what they are doing.

The Great Reunion

There is coming a day when sickness, diseases, death, devastation, and destruction will be no more.

There is coming a day when there will be no more heartache and pain.

There is coming a day when sorrow and mourning will be no more.

There is coming a day when death, the great human separator, will finally come to an end.

There is coming a day when emergency rooms and hospital visits will be a thing of the past.

There is coming a day of a great and grand reunion, when those who die in Christ, and await His coming, will be caught up to meet Him, the host of angels, loved ones who are resurrected, and those living who are translated in the air.

As children of God, one might ask these important and pertinent questions, "What is our role in all of this? Didn't the good book say if we fail to do what we are supposed to do, He will raise up sticks and stones and even the rocks are likely to cry out?

Isn't it to live the life of a child of God, be a witness to others and do everything as lies within our power to ensure we and others are saved in God's Kingdom when He returns to gather His children, from the four corners of the globe, home?

The good Master promised that one day His children from all ages and all walks of life will be caught up to meet Him in the air.

How so comforting, that one day soon we will nevermore part again.

We can't over emphasize or repeat it enough. Oh, what a day when we will first be reunited with Our Great Master and Teacher, Jesus Christ.

Oh, what a day when we will all be reunited with loved ones who lived for Jesus and have long passed,

When all the angelic host of heaven and the unfallen people from other planets will all come together in one accord.

What a joyous and jubilant occasion that will be!

When time without end we will tell the story of Moses, of the Lamb, and how we overcame and made it to the Promised Land.

Nevertheless, until that day, take courage, take heart, and be assured that all those tears that you and your loved ones shed were not in vain.

On this day, while we are still above the ground and probation lingers, let us pledge to our Creator, remaining loved ones, friends, and well-wishers that we will be in that grand and glorious reunion never to part and live in bliss throughout the ceaseless ages of eternity.

Reason for Writing This Poem

Every religion or belief system throughout history and the world believes in the afterlife. They might have different versions of it and how it will take place. For instance, when I studied history and zeroed in on the different cultural practices, I found that many people buried their loved with the nicest and even most expensive apparel and jewelry, items that they loved and cherished, wives, people who assisted them in their homes, etc. But if you talk to many people, regardless of their belief system, they will tell you that one day they would like to be reunited with their loved ones who have passed. We look forward to that day once Christ returns. Every one of us has lost a loved one at some point in life. We all long to see the day when we will meet them again. We all have reunions, whether it is a family reunion, one with old friends and acquaintances, or even schoolmates. It is usually a time to get together and discuss the good, the bad, and the ugly. But the best reunion is being able to meet our loved ones who have passed, especially the ones who have impacted us the most. It is also worth knowing that there is a better world coming and all of us can be a part of it. This poem seeks to capture the essence of it all.

Revisionist History
(Standard English Version)

All they are talking about is revisionist history,
All they are talking about is revisionist history,
All they are talking about is revisionist history!
They say we would be better off if we did not get independence.

All they are talking about is revisionist history,
All they are talking about is revisionist history,
All they are talking about is revisionist history!
They failed to acknowledge the fact that many of our forefathers and mothers put their lives on the line and even died to make this day possible.

All they are talking about is revisionist history,
All they are talking about is revisionist history,
All they are talking about is revisionist history!
They weren't around when it happened and they don't take the time to look it up on Google, Bing, Wikipedia, or even go to the library. Even if you must look it up in an encyclopedia or history books,
Instead they twist and turn the stories to suit their own whims and fancy.

All they are talking about is revisionist history,
All they are talking about is revisionist history,
All they are talking about is revisionist history!
It's time for them to talk to the elders and older heads and learn a thing or two before they jump to conclusions and make up false stories.

All they are talking about is revisionist history,
All they are talking about is revisionist history,
All they are talking about is revisionist history!
Saying we would be better off under the British, is like saying life would be better off if we still used horse-drawn carts, buggies, and wind propelled ships.

All they are talking about is revisionist history,
All they are talking about is revisionist history,
All they are talking about is revisionist history!
So, I'm sick and tired of the revisionist history.

Time for us to learn from our history—
Don't repeat the same mistakes of the past, move forward and bring us back from where we have always been, though small and miniscule in some people's eyes, but tallawah in every sense of the word.

It's time of us to put aside all this revisionist history talk.
Move forward and build this little but powerful island of ours
for everyone living at home, the diaspora living overseas,
Not to mention our visitors and well-wishers who travel here
from time to time from all over the globe.

Revisionist History

(Jamaican Creole "Patois" Version)

All dem a deal wid a revisionist history,
All dem a deal wid a revisionist history,
All dem a deal wid a revisionist history!
Dem se we woulda better off if wi didn't get independence.

All dem a deal wid a revisionist history,
All dem a deal wid a revisionist history,
All dem a deal wid a revisionist history!
Dem nuh acknowledge the fact, many a wi forefathers and mothers put dem life on da line and even die fi mek dis ya day possible.

All dem a deal wid a revisionist history,
All dem a deal wid a revisionist history,
All dem a deal wid a revisionist history!
Dem wasn't round when eh happen and dem nuh tek de time fi Google, Bing, Wikipedia or go a library. Even to look eh up inna encyclopedia or history books,
Instead dem twist and tun de stories to suit dem own whims and fancy.

All dem a deal wid a revisionist history,

All dem a deal wid a revisionist history,
All dem a deal wid a revisionist history!
Time fi dem talk to the elders and older heads and learn a ting or two before dem jump to conclusion and mek up fake stories.

All dem a deal wid a revisionist history,
All dem a deal wid a revisionist history,
All dem a deal wid a revisionist history!
Saying we woulda be better off under wi former colonizers rule, is like saying life woulda better off if we still use horse-drawn cart, buggy and wind propel ships.

All dem a deal wid a revisionist history,
All dem a deal wid a revisionist history,
All dem a deal wid a revisionist history!
So, mi sick and tired a da revisionist history. Time fi learn from wi history, don't repeat mistakes of the past, move forward and bring us back from weh we always have been, though small and miniscule in some people's eyes, we are talawah inna ever sense of the word.

Time fi put aside di revisionist history talk, move forward and build dis little but powerful island of ours for everyone living a yaad, the rest of da people living abroad, our visitors and well-wishers all over da globe.

Reason for Writing This Poem

While growing up in Jamaica, there has always been an ongoing debate as to whether we would be better off under British rule. In order to adequately answer this question, drawing on my history background, we need to look at it from the social, psychological, political, economic, and other perspectives. From the social perspective, we are likely to take on more of a British aura which could work for or against our own unique cultural qualities. Crime and violence-wise that would be under control as Britain would use all its resources to contain and restrain crime. Psychologically we may feel, some of us, that we are incapable of governing ourselves. With regards to politics, are we saying that our forefathers and mothers died in vain, when they fought and even lost their lives so we can have our freedom? Economically, we would be good, but even with this there are downsides. Dealing in hypotheticals does not help. What we need to do is learn from the past and not seek to repeat it, and in so doing we would not be engaged in revisionist history.

Sellout

Would you sell out your sister for a piece of bread?
Or undermine your brother to get ahead?

Would you sell out your doctor for a pot of stew?
Or do injustice to your nurse just to satisfy the few?

Would you sell out your grandma for a small plate of fish?
Or throw your grandpa under the bus to manifest your own wish?

Would you sell out your aunt committing an injustice?
Or do your uncle in, as if it is normal practice?

Would you sell out your niece to satisfy your own self-interest?
Or do your nephew in to advance your own vicious quest?

Would you sell out your foremothers knowing they have been through the rigors of life?
Or do your forefathers in for an unworthy and devious prize?

Many consider selling out their own a badge of honor;
But it brings nothing more than shame and dishonor.

Many sell out their own for their own guilty pleasure,

But sooner or later everything comes crashing in without any measure,

The result is likely to be destructive, devastating, and deplorable.

So, do not sell out your own thinking it is right,

It will end up into an unnerving, unquenchable, and unthinkable separation and isolation for the rest of your entire life.

Reason for Writing This Poem

While in high school, I took a special interest in many subjects but one of my favorite subjects was history. This came about because of one of our teachers, Mr. Owen. He was in his apprentice year as a teacher, but he made teaching come alive and interesting. For example, he had us put history in song, poem, and even drama. Because of this his entire class did not see history as one boring subject with a great deal of notes and unending information to read, digest, and remember, but a delightful subject to learn. Many of us in his class, myself included, took a special love for the subject and most of the students in his class passed the subject in flying colors even up to the external exam level. Personally, I went on to major in the subject in teachers' college and went on to teach it myself, drawing on the methods and way my high school teacher taught the subject. This poem encapsulates many of the injustices that have taken place and unfortunately are still happening today. We historians have a saying: it is not that history repeats itself, but it is that we as a people seem to forget, and things that happened in the past are likely to happen again with devastating effect unless we learn from the past. It is my wish that those who read, internalize, and digest this poem will get the real essence of what it is saying—to be mindful of all humanity and do what is right, fair, just, and equitable to all people regardless of who they are, where they are from, their status in life, and even those to whom they are connected to or influenced by as we journey in this life and beyond.

Twenty-Two Years of Marriage

A Tribute to My Wife on Our Celebration of Twenty-Two Years of Marriage.

Twenty-two years of marriage is no mean feat,

It takes guts, it takes stamina, it takes all you can endure.

Twenty-two years of marriage is not a walk in the park,

It takes obstacles, it takes disappointment, it takes all you can meet.

Twenty-two years of marriage has its ups and downs,

It takes sticking in there, so in the end you can appreciate your crown.

Twenty-two years of marriage has its fair share of disappointments and achievements,

It takes counting your blessings and giving God thanks, so that if we stick in there, one day, we will certainly be heaven bound.

Twenty-two years of marriage has its good and bad,

But I guarantee you, that if you took an inventory, the good will far outweigh the bad.

Twenty-two years of marriage is not something I would trade,

If I had to do it again, you would be the one that I would choose.

So, as we celebrate twenty-two years of marriage,

Let's thank God for the good times and the bad,

Because these are the things that test our mettle and prove we were meant for each other and belong together for the rest of our lives or until Jesus come.

Stick in there hon, the best is yet to come,

You might not be able to see it clearly now,

Just stick in there and with God's help,

We will see the desired outcome.

Reason for Writing This Poem

It was a proud time when we got married and when our son came into the world. When our son came into the picture, it completely changed our perception of life. Many people who had been married for years and raised children of their own told us, "Child rearing will have good days and bad days. You will have your ups and downs. You will have your fair share of disappointment and realized and unrealized dreams. Sometimes things don't happen as fast as you would like them. One thing that remains constant is that the couples who hang in there through thick and thin are the ones who can look back and say it was well worth it." My main hope in this poem is to encourage couples to start on a good foundation and hang in there despite all the things that will confront you in a marriage.

Don't Judge Me by My Accent

Don't judge me by my skin color; judge me by my intellect.

Don't judge me by my skin color; judge me by my years of experience.

Don't judge me by my skin color; judge me by my qualifications.

Don't judge me by my skin color; judge me on what I bring to the table and how I effect meaningful changes.

Don't judge me by my accent; it's not my fault that I speak the way I do. In fact, it's part of who I am.

Don't judge me based on the place in which I live or grew up;

Judge me based on how I have seized the opportunities presented to me in life,

And made myself someone worthwhile and useful to my community, country, society and world at large.

Don't judge me based on my family-tree; I had nothing to do with it, it's just the channel through which I was brought into this world.

Don't judge me on my wealth or world-wide fame; judge me on how I carry myself and act in humility towards my fellowmen in everything that I say and do.

There is no denying that we all have the same red blood cells running through our veins,

There is no denying that from time to time, we all experience similar struggles, challenges, difficulties, and trying circumstances in life.

There is no denying that we all were born as babes, go through the various stages of life, and eventually return to the earth from which we originated.

There is no denying that we are all interrelated or interconnected in some way, shape or form.

So, let's start judging each other for who we are.

So, let's start showing each other respect, value each other on what we are worth,

And most importantly, the vital contribution we have made to each other and—to a larger extent—the whole human race.

Reason for Writing This Poem

As I speak with people who immigrated to this country, they tell me it takes them a little time to adjust and learn the customs, culture and language of this country. Many of them have a hard time adjusting, not just in this country but in other parts of the world. They become culture-shocked. Many people feel that all immigrants who come to the shore of this country should learn the customs, culture and language immediately. This is especially difficult for people who come from other countries, don't know a word of English, or in instances where English is their second or third language. Students who immigrate to this country find it most difficult to adjust. Many of their classmates often mock, tease and bully them. So, they find it very hard to learn unless they seek outside help or have teachers or professors who are very understanding and try to help them along the way. The main objective of the poem is to say, do not judge people by external factors but based on their internal factors and what they have to offer. If we all stick to this approach and are patient and accommodating with each other, this country and the world will be a better place for all of us.

Marriage Is Not for the Faint of Heart

We are told marriage is not a bed of roses; it comes with thorns and thistles.

We are told marriage is never smooth sailing; it comes with rough seas and oceans.

The truth is, marriage has its good and bad days,

In fact, it's nothing like we see in movies or read in books.

The idea that they live happily ever after is a misnomer;

In marriage and in life, there are bumps, winding roads, slopes, and smooth places.

There are bound to be endless arguments, disagreements, and neither of them will get anywhere.

What they fail to reveal, is that in order to avert a crisis it is often better to walk away when sparks fly and deal with things later when cooler heads prevail.

From the time when two individuals meet and show interest in each other, to the wedding day and the married life, there are challenges.

Two people come together from different backgrounds,

Ideas of doing things are likely to vary, one party might believe their way is the right way, the other might believe otherwise.

Unless, both parties agree to meet together and discuss the matter and reach a compromise,

So, learn to communicate with each other from the get go. Allow each one to give their input.

So, come to an agreement as to which approach or solution is in the best interest of the family and many crises, heartaches, and pain will be averted.

After the wedding, take time to know the likes and dislikes of each.

Through the process of time, you will realize how far to go or not to go to press each other's buttons.

When offspring comes into play, you will realize that you both need to be on one page.

Your offspring will go from mom to dad to see which one will give in to him or her more easily. They will see which parent they can manipulate in order to accomplish their goals.

To avoid this from happening, you both consistently need to be on the same page at all times; if you are not sure be honest with your child or children.

Assure them Mom and Dad will talk things over and arrive at a decision that is in the best interest of the offspring and the family.

Never let your disagreement play out in front of your child or children; thrash out your differences between the two of you behind closed doors.

If you fail to do so, I can assure you your offspring will be scarred for life.

Bear in mind you are leaving an impression on the mind of the fruit of your womb which is likely to remain with them throughout their lives, so be careful with what you do and say around them.

Be conscious of the fact that there is no one book or set of books, while they offer solid and life changing advice, that will capture how you adequately raise one child versus another.

However, draw from these sources the best advice and use it to make your marriage and life more worthwhile and longer lasting.

So, on this big day, celebrate the coming together of two completely different lives, learn to love and appreciate each other as the days, weeks, months, and years go by.

Love, respect, and treat each other well, but do not renege on your promise to be honest and trustworthy to each other at all times.

If any party in the marriage is wrong, admit it sooner than later; apologize and move forward, never mentioning it when there is a dispute or disagreement.

Most importantly put God in the center; do not allow other persons or parties to intervene and cause chaos.

Enjoy each other immensely and may your marriage last forever and endure the test of time.

 ## Reason for Writing This Poem

Marriage is one of the greatest institutions that was ever created. Two of the main institutions coming from the beginning of time are worship and family. Both have their challenges. In marriage, from the moment two people set eyes on each other, fall in love, begin courting, and finally decide to get married they enter many unknowns. To begin with both persons come from two different backgrounds with different likes and dislikes, manner of doing things, and strong ideas and views about things. Courtship is the time to get to know each other and to find common ground. They should try to cover as many bases as possible but it is not humanly possible to cover all grounds. This is the reason why people should not rush to get married or they will miss out on this opportunity. The ceremony itself with all its glitter and glamour, whether it is huge or something small, is usually one day or a few hours. During the marriage itself there are challenges. This is usually when the unexpected happens and the parties involved have to deal with it as they come along. This poem is intended to encourage folks to stick in there during the thick and thin. Don't focus on the negatives. Learn to pick your battles and when sparks start flying, cooler temperaments must prevail. If you have a faint of heart during marriage, then you are likely to end up being separated or divorced. Either you are in it for the long haul, or you will throw in the towel and quit.

A True Maverick Gone, but Never Forgotten

A Special Tribute to Former Senator John McCain on His Recent Passing—A True Maverick of All Mavericks

He came into our lives at a tender age, determined to do something worthwhile to enhance the quality of life for himself, his family, and all of humanity.

He joined the armed forces, fought for his country, and was captured and held as a prisoner of war.

And even though the scars of the battlefield remain with him long after his release, he was proud to defend his country, liberty, and ultimate perusal of peace, joy, and happiness.

He never forgot and fought tirelessly for all those, who like him, have put their lives on the line for country, life, and liberty.

He served in the political arena with distinction and even though he was proud of and oftentimes stood up for his political beliefs, the welfare and well-being of his fellowmen was always on his mind before he cast that final vote.

He reached across the aisle to work with the late Ted Kennedy and other political figures and opponents, not always wanting to toe the party line but put humanity's interest first. No doubt he embraced the mantra of putting people and their interest first over and above everything else, not without its fair share of discussion, dissension, and debate.

He had a sense of humor out of this world, but was stern and reprimanded a lady when she tried to discredit and put his opponent in a bad light while running for the highest office in the land. This act among others will have him enshrined as a human being and gentleman who does not seek to put down others but is willing to take the high road every time.

He epitomized the words of John F. Kennedy in every sense and lived it throughout all his interactions and dealings with humanity. "Ask not what your country can do for you—ask what you can do for your country."

He was willing to join with former President Bush and others to put in place a comprehensive immigration plan but many in his own party and others never allowed it to see the light of day.

And as he leaves us, his work in the political arena and life in general goes on and we all crave that many will take a leaf out of his book and seek to emulate him every step of the way.

His wife and children are upstanding and outstanding people and many of the people from the state of Arizona to which he was born and served with distinction, have nothing unflattering to say and often speak proudly of his achievements at home and abroad.

No wonder he was an analyzer, a thoughtful and calculated man. He weighed and thought things out thoroughly before casting his final vote in the interest of the people he represented, and most importantly put his country and humanity over and above everything else.

He was a true maverick in every sense of the word. So live on MAVERICK, live on, your time on this earth was well spent and your life's work will leave an indelible mark on many generations to come.

Reason for Writing This Poem

Senator John McCain was a prisoner of war (POW). He was a senator from the state of Arizona. He ran unsuccessfully as a presidential candidate. He loved his Republican party, its ideology, and philosophy. He did not mind crossing party lines to get things done on behalf of the state he represented and the country at large. He was considered a maverick in everything he did. One of my former neighbors shared a story with me about former Senator McCain before I relocated from the state of Massachusetts to the state of Georgia. He is originally from Vietnam. Despite everything that happened to John McCain in that country, including being torched, he was instrumental in helping this gentleman to come to the United States of America. This, to me, indicates that he was very forgiving and went over and above to help. I write this poem as a tribute to this great man. It is my hope that people will take a page from Senator McCain's book who passed away a few years ago and put humanity's interests over and above politics.

The Quest to Be the Best

A Tribute to the Jamaican Senior Women's Soccer Team in Qualifying for the FIFA World Cup of Soccer in France, Summer 2019

We're on a quest to be the best,

No matter the opponent, no matter the contest.

We take it one game at a time,

We give it our best and that is all that matters.

We're on a quest to be the best,

We put in the time, training, effort, eat well, and exercise.

Now we seek to reap the rewards of our preparation, resilience, and determination.

From the outset, we seek to do it right, get enough sleep, focus on our goals, and the rest will be ours to keep.

Shout it out near and far; we represent our island, our region, and the world.

The Reggae Boyz did it in 98, now the Reggae Girlz, in the same country will face their feat.

Reason for Writing This Poem

This poem was written as a tribute to the Jamaican Senior Women's Soccer Team. They qualified for the premier soccer game in France in Summer 2019. The final was won by the USA (my adopted country). This was a win-win for me because this small island with a population of approximately three million people as of 2018 has seen in its history both its male and female team qualify for the premier sports event in soccer.

Twelve Noteworthy Original Sayings by the Author to Get You through Life

1. "It is not where you were born or your current situation and circumstances in life that should define or determine who you are; it is where you are destined to be and the end results of your positive and determined actions."
2. "If good, conscientious, and fair-minded people sit back and do or say nothing, bad and evil people will always prevail."
3. "One fleeting moment of pleasure is likely to result in a lifetime of regrets."
4. "Can you afford to keep your dignity when others around you are losing theirs?"
5. "Earthly speaking, all good things must end. Heavenly speaking, all good things will never end."
6. "If you, any country, people, or nation fail to learn from the mistakes of the past, they are bound to repeat them and suffer mitigating and dire consequences."
7. "All we can do is to pray for all our haters, naysayers, supposed dream killers, and all those who desire and hope to see us fall on our face and fail."
8. "Nothing beats a try but an outright failure. Try anyhow. Failure should not be a deterrent but a motivation to see where you went wrong and to redouble your efforts and retry, learning from the mistakes you have made in the past and endeavoring not to repeat them."

9. "Heroes are likely to die young; even if this is the case, their words, actions, thoughts, and deeds will forever live on."
10. "Where you are in life and the circumstances in which you find yourself, should not define you—it's where you are headed that matters in the end."
11. "As pilgrims, people passing through a foreign land, we should treat all humanity fairly and justly, look upward towards heaven, and forward to the second coming of our Lord and Savior, our Redeemer, Jesus Christ."
12. "One of the greatest impediments to any person's success in life is a member of their own family (biological-immediate and/or extended), religious, civic, and otherwise who constantly put up hindrances and obstacles in your way endeavoring at all times to prevent you from achieving your goals, objectives, aspirations, dreams, and ambition in life."

Conclusion

Poetry for Our Times is my debut anthology of poems. It is a collection of poems on varied topics that I have written over several years. It also includes poems that I have written recently. Most of the poems touched on the theme of love, be it love between human beings or love between animals. As a matter of fact, some of the poems are love poems that I wrote to my wife over the years.

I also deal with the topic of showing love and appreciation to the people and things around us and other people in our lives. My poems also seek to inspire people to strive for higher heights in life and to reach their maximum potential. I grew up, was inspired, and often sustained by poems that contain uplifting words. I seek to do the same in all my poems. It is my hope that you, your family, and friends will enjoy these poems and that they will make a difference in all of your lives.

Some Upcoming Titles by Patrick H. Williams

1. *No Apology Necessary* **(Part One Of Three Part Non-Fictional Novel)**
2. *Farmer Hezzy and the Grateful Goat* **(Children's Book)**
3. *The Day Grumpy Met Nice* **(Children's Book)**
4. *Never See, Never Hear, Never Say Anything* **(Children's Book)**
5. *We Have More in Common than You Know* **(Non-Fictional Novel)**

TEACH Services, Inc.
P U B L I S H I N G

We invite you to view the complete
selection of titles we publish at:
www.TEACHServices.com

We encourage you to write us
with your thoughts about this,
or any other book we publish at:
info@TEACHServices.com

TEACH Services' titles may be purchased in
bulk quantities for educational, fund-raising,
business, or promotional use.
bulksales@TEACHServices.com

Finally, if you are interested in seeing
your own book in print, please contact us at:
publishing@TEACHServices.com

We are happy to review your manuscript at no charge.

www.ingramcontent.com/pod-product-compliance
Lightning Source LLC
Chambersburg PA
CBHW040315170426
43196CB00020B/2930